# The Power of a Silent Thought

*(Where Does All The Noise Come From?)*

## KRISTEN PITTMAN

# Contents

## Chapters

# Dedications

To my awesome daughter Krishada (Kay): you never cease to amaze me with your caring and thoughtful acts of kindness. You are such a jewel in my life; I can't image it without you. You have grown to be such an exceptional young lady and I'm forever grateful to call you my daughter. I love you.
Mom

I dedicate this book to my mom Lizzie J. I never knew how much wisdom you've imparted to me until now. I didn't understand a lot of things about our relationship growing up like I do now. I was so selfish in how I thought you were supposed to love me, not realizing that we love people based on the love and support we received from our parents. You demonstrated to me the love you knew how to give. For that alone mom, I'm thankful and I no longer take it personally. I wish you could see me now, just as you asked and prayed I "am that and more". I am forever indebted to you. Thank you for being the best mom a daughter could ask for. You're the absolute best.
Your baby girl, Kristen

To my sister Tedra: you would have been so proud of me. I dream of us having sisterly talks and doing so many fun things together. Days go by and I'm realizing that you may not be here in the physical but in another universe we're laughing together like sisters do. Gone too soon, you have ten grandkids now, I hope that's it. They missed you so much. I often think how happy you would have been expressing your love to all of your grandkids.

They're all unique and special in their own way. So much
I need to tell you. Love you dearly.
Your baby sister, Kristen

To my Brother David: how I missed you so much. I
loved you like no other: you were so smart and you could
fix anything. It makes me cry knowing I will never see
you again. I have a daughter who was born on the day
you died. She is so inquisitive and always wants to know
about you. You were so special to me. You called me
TEN and that made me feel special. Rest easy, my
brother. Oh yea tell my sister-in-law Bonnie, I'm thinking
of her to.
Love you, Ten

# Acknowledgements

I cannot express enough thanks to my girl, my friend, my buddy, my pal, my ride or die, my love and my sister Pamela. You have supported me in everything I ever wanted to do, whether good or bad, you were always there. There has never been a break in our chain; you have remained connected to me no matter what. I will forever be grateful for that. I love you girl.

Latrice B. Camp, girl!!!! So much I can say about you. You left us, (*not happy about that*) you still make me cry when I think of you and all the fun and dangerous things we had done. But we understand your urgency to be with the father. You are definitely missed. Love you forever, RIP.

Michelle, Sandra, Twyla, Teresa, Monte, and Catherine, I love you ladies with every ounce of breath I have. (*Which is a lot you know?*) You guys are my rock. There is no doubt I can call on you and you will come to my rescue. And I'm so thankful to call you all my True friends. I know Michelle probably read the top paragraph and felt some type of way, just know Pamela will never take your place … you're so jealous.

To my family, I love you guys more than you will ever know. My sisters and my only brother, you guys have unknowingly taught me about life and how to press through it, even when I felt powerless I was able to do it. Love y'all to pieces.

To my CG family, you guys are the best ... thanks for always pushing me to keep moving towards God. My appreciation for all of you is immeasurable. CG for life!!!!

Thank you Pastor Wrenwrick (Lady Wanda) Williams, for believing in me and for giving me the opportunity to gain the knowledge I needed move forward in life coaching and public speaking. (*In Pastor Rick voice it's going to be EPIC*)

*I finally stepped out my mother's shoebox into a phenomenal life!*

# Introduction

Have you ever heard the saying "a mind is a terrible thing to waste"? Well, that was me, wasting away, listening to everyone's thoughts and opinions of me until I was brave enough to trade in my "wasting away" mentality. I learned to do things to better serve myself and not others. I started reading books and quotes that stuck in my mind. I want to share several quotes with you that pushed me out of my hopelessness to a feeling of being triumphant:

"For I know the thoughts that I think toward you, saith the LORD, thoughts of peace, and not of evil, to give you an expected end." — Jeremiah 29:11 King James Bible

"The mind is a powerful force. It can enslave us or empower us. It can plunge us into the depths of misery or take us to the heights of ecstasy. Learn to use the power wisely." — David Cuschieri

"Our Subconscious minds have no sense of humor, play no jokes and cannot tell the difference between reality and an imagined thought or image. What we continually think about eventually will manifest in our lives." — Robert Collier

"The answer you seek never comes when the mind is busy, they come when the mind is still when silence speaks loudest." — Leon Brown

"There are no limitations to the mind except those we acknowledge." — Napoleon Hill

"The Ego says, Once everything falls into place, I'll feel peace, Spirit says, Find your peace, and then everything will fall

into place."
— Marianne Williamson

"Whatever you hold in your mind will tend to occur in your life. If you continue to believe as you have always believed, you will continue to act as you have always acted. If you continue to act as you have always acted, you will continue to get what you have always gotten. If you want different results in your life or your work, all you have to do is change your mind."
— Anonymous

"It's time for a change". — Kristen Pittman

## Chapter One

# Overcrowded Mind
*It's Time For a Change*

*It is not what goes into the mouth of a man that defiles and dishonors him, but what comes out of the mouth, this defiles and dishonors him." — Matthew 15:11*

*Ever wonder how something that has no sound makes so much noise? I can hear the whispers in the back of my mind, rumbling like thunder. I can hear the chatter and the clutter having a dialogue about everything that I'm trying to ignore, but the more I try to ignore it, the rumbles get louder and louder. As I try to release the pressure of the loud rumbling or crashing noise it appears to be vibrating at a higher speed than my level of consciousness, overcrowding my mind.*

My mind was so congested and crowded with unnecessary traffic: other people's opinions and judgments about me that were not based on fact or knowledge. I made myself believe that those thoughts and opinions *must* be true. I felt like I had so many things going on that I felt like my mind had fallen into a place of overpopulation. This led to a condition that put me on autopilot, and these thoughts had exceeded the holding capacity of my mind. *"What is autopilot?"* you might ask? It's when you do something without realizing that you're doing it.

The subconscious mind is always on autopilot. We have an ingrained autopilot known as the unconscious mind. It carries out all of the things you don't think about consciously - they happen automatically without your conscious attention. Our Internal processes such as feelings, habits, and behaviors are controlled by the unconscious mind.

Overpopulation of the mind is caused by a number of factors, including unwelcome behaviors that are offensive and objectionable. I had fashioned myself to live in the shadows among condemnation and discontentment for so long that I felt imprisoned in my mind. I couldn't tell the difference between real or make-believe. It all felt so natural. My unpleasant attitude was continuously conveyed through my words and body language, Oftentimes, my attitude was perceived as being sarcastic, cynical, and sometimes angry. That's what was hiding in the corners and closets of my mind.

A crowded mind (or a confused mind) does nothing. Whatever you tell it when it's overpopulated, it does the opposite: it's going to go into overload. When your brain feels corroded, overstuffed, clogged, or paralyzed causing an overwhelming feeling and uncontrollable stress, this is overload.

Stress shows up in different forms. Everyone feels stress - it's a part of life. When daily stressors become so overwhelming that they begin to manifest themselves in physical, emotional, or behavioral problems, stress overload may be the cause. Let's look at stress overload and its symptoms.

Here is an excerpt from Matthew Hick that I thought was very informational:

"Stress overload is caused when pressures at work or home become so intense, or last so long, that you begin to feel overwhelmed and out of control. This happens when the hypothalamus continually releases adrenaline and cortisol into the bloodstream, which causes the body to react by increasing blood pressure and heart rate, opening blood vessels wider to allow more blood to be pumped to major organs, and large muscle groups, and glucose to be released by the liver to increase energy and stamina due to ongoing stress in one's life.

Keeping the body under constant 'alert' can be damaging to the heart, lungs, brain, and immune system. Chronic stress overload can cause serious health issues including high blood pressure, diabetes, heart attack, stroke, and depression. It is a disease that must be treated to avoid long-lasting physical and mental effects on the body.

Stress throws your body out of balance. Though there are two kinds of stress, one of which is detrimental to your health. Your body begins to give off signals that stress overload is beginning, and you may begin to feel the following on a regular basis:

- Anxiety and panic attacks
- Constantly feeling pressured, overwhelmed, or hurried
- Irritability and moodiness
- Stomach ailments
- Headaches
- Chest pain
- Sudden onset of allergic reactions
- Sleep problems
- Overwhelming sadness or depression

If you're unsure what causes stress overload, here are a few more examples:

- Exposure to ongoing violence
- Death or chronic illness of a loved one
- Ongoing problems at work or home
- An inability to relax
- Constant overworking

Anxiety can result from daily stress overload, which can make even the most menial stressor seem overwhelming. Sometimes, a stressful situation can become so severe that post-traumatic stress disorder results. This is a reaction that develops in people who experience such a traumatic event that their body and mind exhibits very serious physical, mental, and emotional symptoms to the stress."

It is so important that we unclog our minds so that we can function in what we call "normal" lives. Here is how to conquer it, if practiced on a daily basis.

Stress overload can be dealt with by learning to slow down and relax a variety of relaxation exercises, and/or new coping mechanisms. Sometimes professional help and/or medication are needed to ease the stress.

Whatever you give your attention to becomes your truth. Everything you think becomes a reality. Follow your inner GPS: "Whenever possible, make a legal U-turn". Follow the directions given to lessen stress overload - no detours. Unload *today* so that you can begin to reprogram your subconscious mind. In order to purge unnecessary stress, we have to learn how to think properly.

### *What is the subconscious mind?*

The subconscious is the part of your mind that is not immediately accessible by your conscious mind. The subconscious functions below your normal level of waking consciousness. Envision your subconscious as a filing cabinet that stores information like every wonderful and traumatic experience you have ever had, habits, skills, etc. In contrast, the conscious part of your mind is responsible for logic, generating thoughts, being proactive, and deciding which path to take. In your conscious mind, all of these functions are completely under your control, unlike your subconscious mind. The conscious mind makes decisions and gives orders to the subconscious mind. Therefore, the subconscious will carry out the directive based on what is <u>programmed</u>, not necessarily what you are requesting.

Your subconscious mind carries out the instructions of your conscious mind without questioning. Within your subconscious lie all your beliefs, including beliefs which keep us bound. For example, "I don't want to get close to this person my heart may get broken…" or "I can't do X because of Y", and habits. Our beliefs and habits control our everyday life.

Were you aware that 88% of your mind is comprised of the subconscious, which you do not actively control? According to Sumeru Mind Power, you only use 12% of your conscious mind on a daily basis.

Therefore, your subconscious mind is at the helm; it's running the ship (you). I used the following four techniques to help with reprogramming the mind. There are so many to choose from, but these worked for me.

## *How to Reprogram Your Subconscious Mind*

Limited beliefs and negative habits can be reprogrammed by using affirmations. The subconscious mind learns through repetition. *An affirmation is a definitive statement asserting that something exists or is true.* Every belief and habit you possess were formed through repetition, and we can implant new ones the same way. The first step toward implanting new beliefs and developing new habits is to know exactly what you really want to have, do, and be.

## Strategy 1: Affirmations

Affirmations are an effective way to plant positive messages into your subconscious. They are one of the most effective ways to change a limited or negative belief. You must be careful of affirmations, as they become self-fulfilling prophecies. If you continuously say "this is never going to work," then it is highly probable that things never will. Repetition of an affirmation changes the neural pathways in your brain over time to produce the new belief.

"We can rewire the patterns in our brain with cognitive behavioral therapy or affirmations. Affirmations change the way our brains are wired and the brain lights up differently." — Dr. Mona Lisa Schulz, MD

## Strategy 2: Visualization

Visualization is a technique that involves focusing on positive mental images in order to achieve a particular goal. It is the ability to vividly imagine something – to "see" it in the mind's eye – before it exists in any physical reality. Steve Jobs had a clear mental image of the iPhone's functions and features before he and his team designed the product. Images have a huge impact on your brain, both consciously and subconsciously. Visualization is a great way to program/reprogram your subconscious mind.

## Strategy 3: Meditation

Meditation plays a vital role in reprogramming the subconscious mind because it helps to still the mind. In this state, your brain becomes more receptive; it becomes fertile ground for whatever you want to "implant" into the mind. Your conscious mind engages in the activities of writing powerful goals, creating a vision state, and developing affirmations. To have those seeds take root and flourish into reality, we have to get those words and images soaked deep into our subconscious mind. Placing yourself in a meditative state is an excellent way to help that process. Regular meditation trains your mind to hold its focus without getting distracted. Over time, meditation helps you become laser-focused.

## Strategy 4: Positive Self-Talk

What are you saying to yourself? What are you thinking about? Use these techniques and using positive self-talks as a tool to reprogram the subconscious mind. On a daily basis, we spend more time talking to ourselves than any other person. Our self-talk dictates our mood, behavior, and guides our choices and decisions. Perhaps the most powerful influence on your attitude and emotions are what you say to yourself, and believe.

From utilizing these four simple strategies, I was able to clear up a lot of the "mind noise" and align with my true nature. I went from a place of confusion to an understanding of the mind and how it functions. I created a business called "Mindset Development" and I am a life coach and public speaker now. I took control of my mind and shifted from a place of over-crowdedness to a place of freedom.

**_Quotes you can apply about the mind to your everyday life:_**

"What we think determines what happens to us, so if we want to change our lives, we need to stretch our minds." — _Wayne Dyer_

"The more you see yourself as what you'd like to become, and act as if what you want is already there, the more you'll activate those dormant forces that will collaborate to transform your dream into your reality."

"Not only do you become what you think about, but the world also becomes what you think about. Those who think that the world is a dark place are blind to the light that might illuminate their lives. Those who see the light of the worldview the dark spots as merely potential light."

"If you believe it will work out, you'll see opportunities. If you believe it won't [,] you will see obstacles."

"Begin with the end in mind. Start with the end outcome and work backward to make your dream possible."

"There is one grand lie — that we are limited. The only limits we have are the limits we believe."

"You don't need to be better than anyone else you just need to be better than you used to be."

— All quotes on this page by _Wayne Dyer_

## Chapter Two

# Stop Playing the Blame Game

*Take Responsibility for Your Actions*

*For as he thinks in his heart, so is he [in behavior—one who manipulates]. Proverbs 23:7 Amplified Bible (AMP)*

I remember growing up in a small town in Dillon, South Carolina, on a dirt road full of potholes. The grass was high, and the old oak tree hovered over our neighbor's yard divided by a fence to keep us out and away from their lovely little family. Regardless of their unwanted decorum in such a small town, we still treated each other like family. Even though I was the youngest of nine, I still remember this deeply discomforted feeling of not belonging. I've always had this compelling conviction of wanting my mother to show me the love and attention I was so desperately longing for, not realizing that she couldn't give me what she didn't have. As a child, I didn't understand that. I would continuously ask myself, I had so many unanswered questions: *Why does she act the way she does? Why doesn't she ever hug me, why can't she tuck me in at night, why can't she walk me to the bus or help me with my homework? Does she even care?* Those words played over and over again in my mind. *Can't she see I need her?* Was I invisible to her? She was so caught up in her own life of trying to take care of all of us that she didn't realize how much I needed her. I felt lost and alone and for the next few years my grades had dropped. I went from being an honor roll student to barely cutting it. I stopped caring about school. And when I was there, I wasn't mentally present. She didn't notice my grades had dropped and I didn't care.

I sought the love and attention in the streets. By the time I was 14 I was hanging out at clubs with my sister and her friends. My mom worked third shift, so as long as I made it home by eight a.m. it didn't matter where I was. Why not? She didn't care anyway, so I thought. I lived the next ten years or more doing my own thing and acting out because I blamed her for not being there and giving me the love I felt I deserved. I was inwardly screaming for her love, but again, she didn't hear me. I blamed her for so many years for why I felt insecure and unstable-minded. Even in my adulthood, still living in the darkness of her past, I couldn't get control of my mind and the depressing noise. It was her fault and I made sure my attitude displayed it. I was angry and bitter and I resented her. It was hard for me to be in the same room with her without having a mental conversation of how much I didn't like her. I was confused and didn't understand what was going on or how to fix it for that matter and the noise in my head told me I had the right to be angry. I held on to the noise, it multiplied and got stronger over the years and I didn't understand why this kept reoccurring. Why couldn't I unscramble all the static and the noise? Why couldn't some people connect with me? I was unintentionally offending people with my assertive tone and directness of my voice. I didn't understand this at the time, besides, there wasn't anything wrong with me - so I thought.

There were was six of us: myself, my siblings and other family members all living in a single-wide trailer. It had three bedrooms and two bathrooms before my brother made some additions to give us more living space. We had outgrown the allotted capacity of a small home. The more he added on, the more boarders moved in. It was like a revolving door - just like the rooms in my mind, one thought after another constantly moving in.

There are a lot of missing pieces I can't recall about my childhood; somehow I managed to suppress them - it's almost as if I didn't have a childhood at all. I vaguely remember having fun playing and running like children do. Strangely, I remember running away several times and building my own domain in the woods behind our house. I was looking for something that would show me some form of love, and building that pretend house in the woods didn't provide it either. As the day ended and the night drew near, I paraded back in the house, wondering if my mom had known I ran away. Nope, she didn't even notice. *"What is it going to take?"* I asked, and my mind once again spoke up. "She doesn't love you", "nobody wants you around", "why don't you leave". I reasoned with the noise and I had considered doing my own thing so I ran away again. This time I went further down the street. I had been gone all day - my friends laughed and teased me and called me names, but I was so determined I wasn't going back. As the day ended and the night drew near again, I paraded back in the house and to my amazement, she didn't notice again. I'm running out of options - where could I go next? I'm only supposed to go over to my neighbor's house. I'm only a little girl seeking her mother's love - what is so hard about that?

As I think back, I have no recollection of my mom and I spending quality time together or going to the park, or something as simple as riding to the grocery store. Is it because she didn't drive? Could it be she didn't have her own transportation? Well, tell *that* to an eight-year-old who is starving for her mother's love and have not a clue as to who her daddy is. I found out who my real dad was when I was in the eighth grade: my sister decided to tell me because the older I got, the more I began to look like him. Some things you just don't understand. I have his smile and some of my temperament came from him. I often wonder had I known him growing up if my life would have been any different. Probably not. Just because I didn't know who he was doesn't mean he didn't know about me. He had his own family and we weren't a part of it. Sometimes parents make decisions that affect the whole family. It surely influenced mine.

I remember when I was maybe nine or ten years old, still seeking my mother's love. I would cling to anybody who showed me affection. One summer we had a family member come to town to visit and like most children, you're so excited to see family you hadn't seen in a while, so I immediately clung to him, so close to when we went to bed, I slept in the same bed with him. Why not, I called him Uncle XXX? Well, that night lying in the bed he decided to touch me between my legs, I didn't respond because I didn't know what to do or say. He then lay on top of me and begin to move. I laid there like I was dead. I didn't know what else to do. Thankfully he didn't sexually molest me, but mentally he did. I never told anybody that story because I said to myself, "you should have never gotten in the bed in the first place". He died some years later. They found his body in a river. They never found out who killed him.

Although all these things happened to me, I have no emotion. I feel numb. I am not sure how I'm supposed to feel about it. I have felt shame and guilt for my behavior over the years, and I think that's what kept me stuck for so long - trying to hide from what had happened to me and unconsciously I played it out in accepting whatever attention I could get. No one wanted to claim me, so I accepted second best.

We played fun games in the street and because I wasn't good enough to play and win the insults got worse. We were only doing what most kids do, right? We bullied each other and laughed because it just felt right. I can still remember playing kickball and nobody chose me to be on their team. I was always the last one to be chosen. *I'm only a child, why are these things happening to me? Am I bad? Am I not pretty enough? Am I not smart enough? Why?* I repeatedly asked the noise in my mind, and it was sure to reply "Nope, you're not".

I went through an identity crisis for a very long time. Outwardly I seemed to be okay, but the silent thoughts were talking back to me and I listened. Everything it told me I wasn't. I agreed with it, and then I started repeating what it was telling me, it sounded true, so I aligned with it. I was living in everybody's shadow. Being the youngest of my siblings, I had some really big shoes to fill. I wasn't taught the correct method on how to think like a leader or as someone of great distinction.

Sometimes I felt like I was raising myself by watching all of them live their lives the best they knew how. They all seemed to turn out successful in their own capacity. Still seeking love, I remember when I was in the third or fourth grade, I used to sit my nephew Phillip all the time - I loved him so much it was like he was my baby. The love I had for him was like I had given birth to him myself. I bathed him, I fed him, I dressed him, he slept with me. I took care of him. I had opened my heart to love him despite all the noise and the risk of wanting to be loved.

One day he was outside playing. I can remember the horror like it was yesterday. He was so dirty. I can vividly remember what he was wearing - a pair of black cowboy boots and a green and grey jogging suit, his face smeared with dust from falling on the ground and his nose needed to be cleaned from running around in the cold weather. There was a Caucasian lady from the Department of Social Services who came to take him away so that he could go live with his dad. I was so distraught. I cried and begged them not to take him; I pleaded with them to let him stay. I grabbed him and held him, still begging her not to take him. I washed him up and put him on some clean clothes and they took him away from me. Immediately the noise started again. "I told you nobody cares", it told me, and I agreed that it was true and my behavior changed again.

It was years later before I saw Phillip again. Things just didn't quite feel the same. He didn't remember me and he felt like a stranger to me too. Subconsciously I don't think I ever got over that, it felt like a death. He knows that I'm his aunt, but he has no idea how much I loved him and wanted to keep him. I reached out to him on Facebook, I inboxed him and I wrote on his wall to call me, but he never responded. I wanted him to know just how much I loved him. When the timing is right, we will talk. Looking back and thinking of the person I was, this unexplainable separation might have caused some of my inappropriate and sabotaging behavior.

All of that stored-up anger had caused me to lash out at people. I was so angry and afraid of being hurt that I had developed an unhealthy pattern of trying to hold on to people who didn't want to stay. Those sabotaging patterns of fear, hurt, and feeling unloved cost me some relationships. Built-up anger shows up in different ways. Not only was I lashing out, I had an extreme case of road rage. I had it so bad that I would scream, fuss, and blaspheme, and, depending on how my day was going, I would sometimes pull up beside them and go off again. It was *their* fault that I reacted angrily. In my mind, nobody could drive, or something they were doing caused me to lash out and say things that a Christian woman wouldn't necessarily say, especially in the church world. Not everybody saw this side of me, but if you crossed me or said something to hurt me, the noise started and the anger reared its ugly head. You see, we can only give out what's implanted inside of us. It can show up in patterns of moderation or severity, depending on the situation at hand.

It's like squeezing a lemon to make lemonade: you can squeeze that lemon delicately with a juicer to get juice or you can cut it all up, squeeze it roughly, etc. You're only going to get lemon juice.

It didn't matter how you squeezed me, you were only going to get anger, hurt, and bitterness because that was what was prevalent inside me. It was vibrating at a high frequency and it affected a lot of people in a negative way.

I lived with the noise for a long time and when I got around certain people I camouflaged myself because I didn't want them to see how I was trying to resist the silent and angry thoughts. I made myself believe that if I showered them with gifts they would like or accept me, so I started to nurture this behavior with everybody I met. It seemed to work as long as I was buying the gifts, but at the same time, I was being talked about by the same people I was buying gifts for. It's funny how we accept something on one side while rejecting it on another. I was screaming for help and no one heard me. Could it be they were screaming for help too? I was showing all the signs of having abandonment issues but no one picked up on it or had any knowledge of what I needed to change, not even in the church. I'm not criticizing the church, but sometimes no one can see what you need internally. It was easier for me to place blame on others, so I blamed my mother.

"The phrase 'a mind is a terrible thing to waste' comes to mind here." I was wasting my life away, blaming everyone for the noise in my head. I didn't know I could take responsibility for my actions, so I didn't. It was easier to blame someone else for how I was feeling.

Growing up, I got teased a lot - that was part of the noise in my mind that made that thundering sound. It was silent to those around me, but it was very loud to me. I thought I wasn't pretty enough, loved enough and listening to those thoughts my body surely was heavy enough. Bullies called me "flat butt" for so long, I started saying it and I believed it. It was certain clothing I wouldn't wear. Any clothing that was tight and would show my "flat butt" I would definitely stay away from. Those two powerful words controlled the rest of my life: (*What is controlling your life*) it plagued me so much that I placed my value of who I was on that statement, especially in relationships. I didn't think I "had it", so to speak, that reflected the type of men I chose. In turn, they didn't think I was worth much either. Those words would always play on repeat in the back of my mind. The worse it got, the more I blamed my family and friends for infusing that type of belief in me. Of course - they were the ones who said it, right?

Sometimes we don't know the impact we will have on a person's life. It's imperative that we speak uplifting and encouraging words to people around us. I had listened to those silent thoughts for so long I adopted a life of low self-esteem and had no self-love. I lost some really good relationships with men because I didn't know how to behave appropriately. I unknowingly sabotaged some of my relationships out of fear of rejection or denial. I wasn't conscious of the negative energy I was giving off, so it ran them away. I would talk too much about nothing or my tone and demeanor were unpleasant or unfriendly. If that didn't do it, I displayed myself in a desperate or impulsive manner. Yet again, this was someone else's fault, since I didn't get what I needed growing up - or so I thought.

Take a look at this passage:

"Now there is at Jerusalem by the sheep market a pool, which is called in the Hebrew tongue Bethesda, having five porches. [3] In these lay a great multitude of impotent folk, of blind, halt, withered, waiting for the moving of the water. [4] For an angel went down at a certain season into the pool, and troubled the water: whosoever then first after the troubling of the water stepped in was made whole of whatsoever disease he had. [5] And a certain man was there, which had an infirmity thirty and eight years. [6] When Jesus saw him lie, and knew that he had been now a long time, in that case, he saith unto him, Wilt thou be made whole? [7] The impotent man answered him, Sir; I have no man, when the water is troubled, to put me into the pool: but while I am coming, another steppeth down before me. [8] Jesus saith unto him, Rise, take up thy bed, and walk."

— John 5:2-8, King James Bible

Here is a great example of someone blaming others for why he can't get in the pool. So often we blame others as to why we are where we are: mentally, emotionally, or physically. Concentrate on the 8th verse. Stop blaming others for your handicap and take up your bed and walk. Reading and understanding that passage encouraged and inspired to write this book. I took up my bed of "the Blame Game" and began to proceed to the high route to freedom.

If we keep listening to the noise and thinking that someone caused hurt or misunderstandings, you will be waiting your whole life for someone to come and remove it - like I did for years. Waiting for my mother to act in a loving way or say all the right things to me so that I could feel better and okay about who I had become: a dark, clouded person on the inside. Externally, I was searching for acceptance and approval from people. I was craving that validation that no one could give me. I realized that it was already within me: it was buried underneath all the clutter and sounds of thunder and rumbling I had created in my mind.

I remember preparing to teach at my church one Sunday morning, still waiting on validation, I wanted someone to say or give me permission to be me. While I was preparing, I begin to ask the Lord to help me. I was in the first chapter in the Book of Genesis, where it speaks about being created in the image of God. I felt this repulsive brokenness on the inside and I couldn't shake it. It was at that moment that God spoke and said, "*NO ONE WILL EVER BE ABLE TO PUT A STAMP OF APPROVAL ON SOMETHING I CREATED*. They aren't qualified." That was the best news I had heard in a very long time. And from that day, wanting and looking for approval stopped. "Finding freedom is free".

This strange but familiar echo that kept coming from a far place: "You can't do it", "You don't deserve it", and "you're not worthy to have it", and I can't forget the one that haunted me the most: "flat butt". We've all heard those loud echoing sounds before: far away, but powerful enough to penetrate through all the rooms of your mind.

I kept going back to when I was 5 or 6 years old or younger, my mom working different shifts and having hired a babysitter. His name was Mr. June. He would keep us while our mom worked. I can remember on some days he would call me and my sister Tedra in the room he was in. We would be running around in our t-shirts and underwear, and he would open up our panties and stick his hand in and play with us, then send us back out to play. Why would my mom allow this to happen to us?

After years of feeling unworthy, I finally came to the realization that I was not my mother. I could no longer live up to anybody else's expectations of me. I could no longer cheat myself out of this eminent life that God had designed me to live. You see, I finally realized what I had been doing all along. I sought out to find a better way to live, which meant I had to change the way I had been thinking.

I started researching the mind and how I could use my mind to work for me and not against me. The more I learned, the more I was enlightened on what I was learning about my conscious and subconscious mind.

In February 2014 my mom had a major stroke which left her paralyzed on her left side. My mom was a tough lady - she loved hard and she was very independent, so I knew when this had happened it wasn't going be good for her. She always told us that if anything happened to her and she wouldn't be able to take care of herself, she didn't want to live that way. She unintentionally taught me how to be strong so when she got sick I expected her to be the same way. Unfortunately, that wasn't the case at all: mentally and emotionally she chose not to stay on this side of the earth so just in a short while her life ended on April 10th. That added to my mental chatter, and I grew even more furious because she didn't fight to stay here with me. *Why would she leave me without giving me instructions on how to live without her?* I asked myself this question for months, and the more I thought about her leaving me, the angrier I became. I was so mad at her for so many different reasons, but the number one reason was that I felt she gave up. Maybe that was selfish of me, but I thought for years she was selfish too for not "correctly" loving me. I had unconsciously assembled my whole life piece-by-piece by surveying her every movement, only to realize I had aborted so many pleasures because I mirrored her. It wasn't her fault - she was only doing what most of us do: replicate what we've seen.

Going forward, it's now the year 2016. I'm in the process of learning how to think right and live according to my true self. I had to undo some important things that I had done wrong in the past. I had rubbed some people the wrong way and I needed to go back and make things right. That started with the act of forgiving. One of the people I needed to forgive was my mother. Regrettably, she had transitioned two years prior so I had to think of another way to release anything and everything that would stop me from moving forward, so I wrote her a letter:

Mom
   I forgive you for not giving me the full guidance I needed to succeed in life. I also forgive you for not knowing how to love me when I needed your love and attention. I forgive you for not teaching me the value of self-worth and acceptance. I understand you were never taught love and affection so you could only give me what your mom gave you.
   I love you now just for being the mother you knew how to be. I appreciate all you have taught me, you taught me how to be a great cook and an awesome decorator, and I wish you could see what I have done since you were here last. I'm self-sufficient, strong-willed, determined to get the job done, and I credit that all to you.
   Thank you for all you've done because it made me the woman I am today.
   I love you, your baby girl Kristen

Writing this letter felt great and I felt the sincerity as I wrote it. A few days have gone by and I wanted to read it again. It felt so real that it was then, in that moment, I realized all this time I listened to my silent thoughts, I had attributed all my successes and all the good things I had ever done to myself, I told myself, "I was the one who made it happen". But something inside of me felt unusual - different this time. I had an epiphany. It dawned on me that all of my successes and all of my strengths were only because of her: my zeal for life, my tenacity for not giving up, my strength to overcome, my dedication, my ambition, my detail for decorating, my love of cooking, being a great mother, the act of being able to listen, and the practice to coach others. It was all because of my mother. Suddenly my mind was beginning to be rewired with the good stuff, and I was enjoying how it made me feel.

As you begin to clean out the rooms of your mind, you run into other things you leave undone. I had truly not forgiven my sister Tedra, for how I thought she behaved toward me. I'm not saying everything was my fault; in this book, I will only talk about why we couldn't see eye-to-eye. I had to make that right too, as she too had transitioned almost nine years prior from health issues that had taken her life.

One part of changing the way you think is clearing all forgiveness from your mind and heart. While I was on a roll of correcting what I felt I had done wrong, I also wrote her a letter to release it all:

Tedra,

I forgive you for not understanding the bond between sisters because we weren't properly taught the true meaning of love. You didn't know. I forgive you for all the times we allowed the simplest things come between us. Thank you for being my sister for a short time here on earth. You gave me 4 beautiful and talented nieces and one handsome and smart nephew. Thank you for all the times we did talk and laugh

together, one thing for sure, you loved God and he adored and loves you too.
P.S. Tell my brother, we sure miss him...sending kisses to the three of you.
Gone too soon,
Your baby sister Kristen

Forgive yourself for all the past mistakes you have made. Begin to look at every negative occurrence that has happened to you as an opportunity to do it better the next time. Look at every failure and problem as a possibility to improve. Make your "BUT's" work for you, not against you. I'm feeling a lot better, and it only gets better.

As you begin your journey of changing - your thoughts, behavior, attitude, and the way you go about life - pure thoughts will begin to fill your mind and you will want to show the world just how much progress you've made. You will have this excitement that is unexplainable and you will want to share it with everyone you interact with. You will encounter some resistance as you change the way you use to do things. Adopt on the IDC syndrome: an "I Don't Care" attitude and keep moving forward. Congratulations on your next level!

**Quotes about taking responsibility you can apply to your everyday life**

"Usually making excuses is just something we can get away with, rather than challenging or changing ourselves. If we want to change and we want our life to work at a level you've never had before, then take responsibility for it." – *Wayne Dyer*

"Everything you do is based on the choices you make; it's not your parents, your past relationships, your job, the economy, the weather, an argument or your age that is to blame. You and only you are responsible for every decision and choice you make…Period." – *Wayne Dyer*

"Blame is a neat little device that you can use whenever you don't want to take responsibility for something in your life, use it and you will avoid all risks and impede your own growth." – *Wayne Dyer*

"Enlightenment demands that you take responsibility for your way of life." – *Wayne Dyer*

"Taking responsibility for being exactly where you are gives you the power to be exactly where you want to be."
– *Author Unknown*

"The more you take responsibility for your past and present, the more you are able to create the future you seek". – *Unknown*

"Responsibility is the price of freedom". – *Elbert Hubbard*

# Chapter Three

# Shifting From Selfishness to Servitude
## Show Gratitude

*"Don't pick on people, jump on their failures, and criticize their faults— unless, of course, you want the same treatment. Don't condemn those who are down; that hardness can boomerang. Be easy on people; you'll find life a lot easier. Give away your life; you'll find life given back, but not merely given back—given back with bonus and blessing. Giving, not getting is the way. Generosity begets generosity."* Give and it shall be giving unto you, Luke 6:38 The Message (MSG)

"Practice being kind instead of being right."
– Wayne Dyer

Regardless of the noise spinning in my mind, serving and giving are my strong points. This was something that came naturally. Ironically, I had no problem doing it. Even through the noise and my misguided thoughts, giving was one of the qualities I over-indulged in because I didn't know how to balance what was real and what was imaginary from the noise in my mind. I tricked myself into thinking I was hiding my weaknesses and shortcomings, but I was actually exposing them in various forms.

38

I love to give even when I give for all the wrong reasons. I gave under false pretenses, which allowed others to take advantage of me being nice. I gave foolishly, and, even when I couldn't afford to give, I gave anyway. I was strong-willed and determined. I would have done anything not to appear weak; I did everything and anything with great aspiration and motivation, trying to prove a point that no one was interested in anyway. I learned how to show gratitude at an early age - not because I watched others do it, but because that was the one thing that got a positive reaction and it seemed to be the only thing working in my favor. Everybody likes gifts, right? Showing gratitude allowed me to be thankful for a lot of things - even the little things like saying "thank you" and acknowledging when someone did something nice or good. I like that feeling, so I wanted to do more. It wasn't until later on in my adulthood that I started experiencing the shift from selfishness to servitude. It took me a while to realize what was happening.

In 2009, I lost my job as an X-ray technician making good money. I had acquired a lot of things: I had bought my first home, two cars, and I was doing well for myself. I was able to take at least 2 vacations a year, and between them I still traveled and did things I liked to do. I wasn't rich by the world's standards, but I lived well - so I thought. It's funny how we can live well but still unknowingly carry a poverty mindset; strangely, there were a lot of things I needed to learn and money couldn't buy them. Sometimes life experiences change the way you see things and make you reevaluate what's important and what's not.

I've been on both sides of the spectrum of employment. People treat you like you have a disease when you're unemployed - it's like you're infectious and they're afraid you'll spread the deadly unemployable virus, so they avoid you. I experienced this and I felt lonely and abandoned again. Losing my job set me back mentally and emotionally. The noise started again: this time it was a different noise, a noise of self-pity and deep despair, but it was only temporary. I went from having two cars to not having one for six long months. Six months is a long time to go without a car, especially when you're used to having two parked in your garage. During this time, I'm so grateful for one of my brothers in the church, Brother Ted, he took me everywhere I needed to go for six months. He never complained and oftentimes would call and ask if I needed to go anywhere. He never made me feel like I was a burden to him and that meant everything to me. He made me feel at ease so I didn't think about the fact that I didn't have transportation, because I always had it with him. I will never forget what he did for me and I'm going to bless him for what he did. I had a dream that I wrote him a check for $250,000.00 and I look forward to the day I can do that for him - he is more than deserving of it. My daughter calls him "pa pa" and I have adopted the name as well. God sent me an angel when I needed it the most. Thanks, my brother.

I remember when I was desperate to get a car that I called up my mom and asked if she could co-sign for me - my credit didn't meet the standard because I had lost my job - the car was only six thousand dollars and I was going to make a down payment of two thousand dollars. I wanted that car so bad. Well, that didn't happen; not because she didn't want to, but other circumstances threatened her not to do it. When you are under someone else's control, life is different. I often think of that situation and I remind myself if it was me and my daughter needed my help, I would have done what was necessary. I learned this from that situation to trust God and know that sometimes he allows things to happen, or doors to close, so that He can get all the glory out your life. He had a plan for me and I all had to do was trust him. About a week later I found a car and didn't need anyone's help - God did it and no one could take the credit for something He did. We may not always understand why things happen the way they do. Just know that you have a greater one who wants the very best for you. Not only did I lose my car, but I was also facing foreclosure and the bank was threatening to take my home multiple times during the years I didn't work. The only thing I had to hold onto was a confession I had made years prior, that "my house was paid in full", and every time I got those foreclosure sale date papers in the mail, I said "God, you told me my house was paid in full". This wasn't easy and I had my moments, but I never let go of HIS promise. And I kept my house. It's been twelve years since I moved in and things began to turn around for me.

My image never changed and had I not told anyone what I was going through. They would have never known it - I still had my million dollar smile (*it's what saved me*) and I continued to serve and give. The only income I had was child support. It was less than what I needed to survive - yet my daughter and I ate every day, my lights never got turned off, my phone bill was paid every month, and I was happy, even through all the noise. I refused to give up. I held my head up high even when I felt like I was a burden to some. Pride didn't stop me this time, because I knew I needed help, you find out that everybody isn't always willing to help. Some make you feel like you are a liability because you need help and when you finally got up the nerve to ask; they'll say no or not respond at all. Boy, did I experience this especially from family! Not all, but some. Now, I'm not talking about this because I'm holding any kind of grudge - I love my family - but this is just part of my story.

In the neighborhood I live in we have a Housing Association that requires dues every month. When I lost my job, I fell behind in my monthly dues and couldn't catch up. I had written letters to the Association asking if I could make payments; the answer was "no". I even mailed them a check for part of the arrears only to have it returned because they wanted full payment and I didn't have the full amount so they threatened to put me out. To make a long story short, I later received a letter in the mail from an attorney's office stating that if I didn't pay them $3,500 in a week that they would padlock my home. Well, I didn't have the money and didn't know who to ask. On the day they disclosed, they came and padlocked my home and made me leave. My daughter was currently at school so she didn't know at the time.

I was a mental wreck. (*The noise began*) Emotionally still believing in God for a miracle and having no money to pay the fee. I immediately called a few family members - one said she had it, but didn't want to touch it as she was going through a divorce, and she made the comment that I might not be able to keep my house. I called another - she never responded to my distress. One sister tried to help me think of someone who may have had the money to give. But still, no luck.

Parked in my sister's driveway, I cried wondering how I was going to pull this off. I was embarrassed, beyond hurt, and I felt horrible. *What will I tell my daughter?* At that moment my phone rang, and I will never forget that day. Tasheva said, "What's wrong auntie?" I explained to her what was going on and she asked how much do you owed, where do I need to send the money, and to stop crying. "You've been in your house too long to lose it over $3, 500," she said. "I will send you the money". (*She never asked what did you do wrong or how did you get to this place, she asked no questions*) She left work and wired the money to me. Even as I type this, I still cry because she has no idea how much that meant to me. And one day soon I'm going to bless her. I paid her every dime back but I have so many blessings that I am going to shower her with, and that's a promise. When people show up for you when you need them the most, they are like angels God sent to help you. She was definitely my angel that day. To this day I still thank her for what she has done for my daughter and me. Ta-Sheva L. Pouncey, I thank God for you.

Through this transition of loss, I never stopped serving and giving. Giving isn't always monetary; sometimes it's your time and encouragement that you give to make people feel better. That was something I was great at and I loved doing it. It's easy to give out of abundance - try doing it when there is a *lack* of something and you're still required to give. That didn't stop me. I remained faithful and kept a great attitude. Well I'm stretching it a little but I had improved a lot.

Giving is an act of kindness: it evokes gratitude and it makes you feel happy - not just for the receiver, but for you, too. Whether you're on the giving or receiving end of a gift, it elicits feelings of gratitude. It is a great way of expressing gratitude and God loves those who have a heart to give.

Showing gratitude was the only positive thing I cultivated and nurtured during my adolescent days, primarily because I was searching for love and I found it in giving. When we show gratitude on a daily basis, it increases personal happiness in us and in the lives of others. When gratitude is expressed it boosts positivity within yourself and others.

Giving is like any other positive emotion, making one feel free and open to explore new ways to participate. It's contagious, and, if done with the right motive, it can spread from heart to heart. Serving is a part of life, and a form of giving: just about everything we do requires us to serve. Giving and serving goes hand in hand - you can't have one without the other. Serving should be one of our greatest qualities, exemplifying the heart of who we are for helping others in so many different ways. It makes you smile, and you get so much joy from seeing how you made someone else smile.

Gratitude is a powerful weapon: it opens doors that you just can't explain. When situations in your life happen that you can't explain, or, maybe when you desperately needed something, it will appear or someone may have called and gave just what you needed. God is an on-time God.

Serving and giving should always be done with the right motive (*not to be seen or tempted to build ourselves up in the eyes of friends or family*); we should humbly serve others and do it with a pure heart. One of the many things that stop us from giving and serving others is a *"what about me" attitude"*.

There were a lot of things I could have given my attention to when I felt like I didn't have enough, but I wanted to focus on what I was good at and that was giving and serving, so I purposely made that my focal point. It's so easy to focus on the things that aren't going right, things that you need, things that you don't have; lack, brokenness, anger, or bitterness, but I decided to concentrate on doing something good and it made me feel good to know that I was finally doing something right and with the right intention.

No matter where you are in life, make a decision to give and serve others. Give free and freely, no charge, and watch how things miraculously happen for you; it did for me. I still live in my home and I have two cars parked in my garage. Give and it shall be given unto you!

## *Here are some gratitude quotes to ponder:*

"Feeling gratitude and not expressing it is like wrapping a present and not giving it." – *Practical.com*

"Gratitude is one of the sweet shortcuts to finding peace of mind and happiness inside. No matter what is going on outside of us, there is always something we could be grateful for." – *Cicero*

"To educate yourself for the feeling of gratitude means to take nothing for granted, but to always seek out and value the kind that will stand behind the action. Nothing that is done for you is a matter of course. Everything originates in a will for the good, which is directed at you. Train yourself never to put off the word or action for the expression of gratitude." – *Alfred Painter*

"Revenge is profitable, gratitude is expensive." – *Eric Hoffer*

"Be in a state of gratitude for everything that shows up in your life, be thankful for the storms as well as the smooth sailing." – *Wayne Dyer*

"See the light in others, and treat them as if that is all you see." – *Wayne Dyer*

"Gratitude is riches, complaints are poverty." – *Wayne Dyer*

# Chapter Four

# Learning How to be Authentic
## *Show Up As Yourself*

*Do not be conformed to this world, but be transformed by the renewal of your mind, that by testing you may discern what is the will of God, what is good and acceptable and perfect. Romans 12:1*

Authentic simply means real or genuine - not copied. I'm sure you've heard the phrase "be yourself, everyone else is already taken" by Oscar Wilde. *Why am I afraid to be my authentic self?* Is a question I asked for years, plagued with everybody's opinions of what I should be or should be doing? I lived over half of my life hiding behind a pretense of who I really was. *Pretending is so obsolete.*

I tried to express my authentic self, but was rejected time and time again. I didn't quite understand why I wasn't accepted, (*The noise had told me many reasons why*) so I just adapted to what felt "right" to deter any disapprovals of who I was trying to be. Either I didn't say it right, my body language was wrong, or I was unapproachable; I was rude or mean and my tone was too authoritative. I didn't know how I was supposed to conduct myself and I had too many people living in my mind. I acted one way with this crowd, acted another way with that group, just to try and not offend anyone at all while at the same time transgressing against myself. I was uncomfortable in my own skin. I would try and talk softly thinking that would help. It didn't. I would straighten up my face, trying not to look like I wasn't mean-mugging, that didn't work either. I would change up my words, use words I thought would be more inviting, and that didn't work either. I was running out of ways to appeal to their selfishness. Yes, selfishness!

We want people to act a certain way so that we can be okay. We ask people to present themselves in an acceptable manner so that *we* can feel good about *ourselves*. That's selfish! No matter how a person conducts themselves, it shouldn't change who *you* are.

Because of this type of performance, (*Academy award winner*) I grew angrier on the inside because I didn't know how to break loose of everybody's judgments.

On my journey towards a more authentic self, I started looking up the definitions of words I was called -"mean" and "rude" they stuck out the most. To my surprise that didn't define me I wasn't that at all. Let's look at the meaning behind these words:

1. *Mean is lacking in kindness, unkind, or bullying.*
2. *Rude is offensively impolite or ill-mannered.*

I realized - that I had answered to that all my life! I had believed this about myself for so long-because of the people, who had spoken those words; I was [admittedly] unaware and ignorant of what those words meant. Sometimes we say things to people that we don't know ourselves. Let's look at the man in the mirror.

48

I knew I needed to set some boundaries. Unfortunately, I didn't know the first thing about doing that, so I continued to allow others to control my actions while sabotaging my own happiness. It became such a ritual; I felt stuck in this maze of my refusal to say "no", putting everybody's needs before my own, and worrying about how they felt about me. There I was, an outspoken and strong person, too scared and fearful to stand up for herself because she didn't want to confront the image she placed on herself.

I was trying so hard not to be rejected. That would've triggered me to be vulnerable and appear weak, and I could never let that happen. My image was way too influential, or so I thought. The image I was really trying to hide was this fragile little girl. How could I ever let someone see me undress all my flaws reminding me of my childhood nightmares? I was so co-dependent on everybody's opinion; I needed validation so strongly that it was hard to make a decision without seeking what others thought prior to me making it. If they weren't in agreement with me, I wouldn't make the decision. I remember I had an impulse to create a design for a t-shirt, and I was so excited about it. After a few weeks, I finally got the design back and I was ready to share it. When I did, hardly anyone liked it, (I *only asked a few*) so I didn't pursue it further. I never use the design I had visualized in my mind all because I didn't get the results I was hoping for – seeking someone else's permission to be myself. "Free your mind and the rest will follow".

I was living as "Perfect Patty" - everything had to be done right and I realized I was raising my daughter to be the same way. I had pushed her so hard to be perfect and most of the times; I didn't allow her to make a mistake without me reprimanding her. She's a senior in high school now, and it hit me that I was projecting this Perfect Patty behavior toward her. I had to apologize to her and allow her to be who she supposed to be and not what I was trying to make her be. I had to give Krishada back her free will to make her own decisions. I had to learn (*and am still learning*) how to make allowances to her and make her feel safe and that's it's okay to make mistakes. She is totally awesome.

I was so messed up mentally that I built this invisible protective gear to guard myself from people who I assumed would hurt me - prejudging them, I put up a wall to keep everybody out while keeping myself locked in, especially in relationships. I told myself that I didn't like to kiss, shielding myself from intimacy. I refused to consent to feelings of affection and love, I wasn't about to open up my heart; it was only so far I would let anybody in. I displayed this masculine energy for so long I didn't know how to show off my feminine side so I connected with almost every man/person I met from my intellectual mind instead of my heart.

I didn't know how to open up my heart to a man without feeling like he wasn't going to accept me. It was easier to offer him my mind instead - my mind was so congested with everybody's opinions and judgments he didn't want to stay either. I had been hurt numerous times in the past, so I had to learn how to make my heart inaccessible to people. I've never been in love - I thought I had on several occasions but that was just a sense of love based on sexual acts - or someone treating me with kindness. It was never out of a pure heart. I'm learning now what true love is, so when that time comes around again, I will know how to express it the right way.

Setting boundaries is challenging for everyone and it's an area I'm not accustomed to. I have since then set some guidelines for myself to move forward. It's a vital part of becoming who I'm supposed to be.

Authenticity is the quality of being genuine or real - no more pretending or illusions of being someone else.

When I was growing up we use to jump rope a lot and played a game we called "Double Dutch". I didn't do that right either; they called me "sling foot" and laughed at me. I'm still unsure until this day what that meant, but I knew it wasn't a compliment and that I wasn't doing it right according to the others. Every time we would play Double Dutch they called me that, so I didn't want to play anymore. I answered to a lot of names - I became a lot of names - and being authentic wasn't one of them. I didn't know I could be myself, so I didn't.

I was so afraid of rejection that it became something I looked forward to. It seemed like the more I tried to dismiss it, the more I called it to myself. I was sure to meet someone who would reject me; to try and prevent that from happening, I started offering gifts, but unconsciously I was sending out a signal of desperation that would make them leave anyway. This was an ongoing cycle that kept showing up at the most inopportune times. It became a lifestyle and I was sure to present it at whatever cost.

Let's talk about rejection: the act of refusing to accept, to cast off, exclude or withhold from. *Does that sound like your life at some point?* Rejection knows no boundaries; it invades your social and romantic life, and it can even invade your job. It feels awful because "it communicates the awareness to somebody that they're not loved or good enough, or not in some way valued" *Amanda L Chan.*

What we hold little value in we don't appreciate, so we misuse it.

*Have you ever felt misused?* I've experienced this; when we feel like someone has rejected us, the question to ask is: did they reject us, or could it be that they weren't interested in what we have to offer? There's a big difference. People don't reject us – sometimes they're not interested and that's ok. We don't always accept what people offer us. I had to learn the difference between rejection and ignorance. Sometimes they just don't know.

We all have a fundamental need to belong. When we feel rejected or may not fully understand the meaning of rejection, this disconnection we feel can enhance our emotional pain, make us feel alone and possibly have a deep-seated impact on our behavior.

One of the biggest misconceptions of rejection is a romantic rejection. When this happens, it seems like our world turns upside down. We often respond to romantic rejections by finding fault in ourselves - complaining about all our inadequacies, kicking ourselves when we're already down, and degrading our self-esteem as something cheap or trashy. When we blame ourselves by attacking our self-worth only deepens the emotional pain we feel and makes it harder for us to recover emotionally. Before you rush to blame yourself, keep in mind the fact that you are absolutely amazing. There is nothing wrong with you; you were designed fearfully and wonderfully, marvelous you are. As you begin to come into your authentic self, some may be insulted by your new mindset, but don't worry; embrace the evolution of your true existence.

I remember a time when I still wrestled with rejection because I didn't understand what it really meant. I literally felt worthless; I couldn't get past my own thoughts, let alone someone else's. It didn't matter how many times someone told me I was beautiful or pretty. I didn't believe it and my response was always adding something negative behind their compliment. I had it so bad that I didn't know how to reply to any type of praise or approval, at least not in a positive way.

Still trying to find my identity, I went to church one Sunday, knowing I needed help in regaining my sense of worthiness. I went to the place I could get help. At the end of service, I went up for prayer and my pastor's wife asked me to scream. Boy, I thought that was silly and definitely not what I needed! I remember her telling me to imagine I was a broken vase put together without any glue. *Hmmm, what does that mean?* Well, it meant that I could fall apart at any time because there was nothing significant holding me together and what was holding its shape or form together was a bunch of opinions, feelings, thoughts, beliefs, and ideas from people I valued and respected. If any of their convincing opinions or judgments came my way, I immediately would have shattered and my exterior of the broken vase would be misdirected again. The noise in my head was feeding off of all the negativity I was receiving.

Feeling embarrassed to scream, I uttered out the loudest scream. She said to do it again - this time, no shame in my game - I screamed again. I felt this release immediately and for a while, I felt great, felt like I was somebody on a mission to be free. After a while of feeling unrestricted, I began to feel unworthy again. That was because I had not reprogrammed my unconscious mind with words that would inspire. If we don't download the right information to help us develop, it will appear that we've been malnourished and neglected. Outwardly I looked healthy; inwardly I was starving and the lack of good mental nutrition was slowly killing me. It wasn't until recently I found a better diet that I could digest; I started to be reprogrammed.

I started listening to subliminal messages to clear any unwanted behaviors. A subliminal message is a signal or message designed to pass below (sub) the normal limits of perception. It might be inaudible to the conscious mind, but audible to the unconscious or deeper mind. Or, it might be an image transmitted briefly and unperceived consciously but perceived unconsciously. This helped me tremendously and I felt great; I had so much energy and my language had shifted from talking negatively to an encouraging and uplifting momentum. I felt alive again and I was telling everybody I could about my new found authentic self.

Authenticity allows you to live freely in opposition to anyone's approval of you. You don't have to be in competition with anyone - authenticity gives you the courage to be yourself. It allows you to uncover your higher self. So, be true and genuine with yourself. Walk gracefully in your authenticity and watch the freedom you allow in your life. When you present yourself authentically, you create the space for others to do the same.

Authenticity is living the life you love. I used to dread getting up in the morning and going to work, feeling no real reason for going other than a paycheck. When I began my new outlook on life, I changed the energy around me. Now, when I get up for work, I actually look forward to going because it allows me to think freely, walk on my breaks, and talk to my creator or write in my journal as thoughts come to mind. I revel in getting up now. I enjoy the energy that radiates from me being in such a good place. Being authentic allowed me to fall in love with myself. I no longer look in the mirror and dislike what I see. I don't nit-pick about my weight, my size, or my figure anymore. I look into the mirror now and say "I like me." I like being around me. I like my company and I like my physique. I tell myself "you're sexy and beautiful." When I dress up I feel like I'm glowing with confidence and style. I have confidence, and I love it. Being authentic was one of the best decisions I could have made, to show up as myself wherever I go.

Learn how to live free of anybody's opinions or approval. Be the person you were born to be: great and powerful. Start today - show up authentic.

**Here are a few quotes to live by about being authentic:**

"Freedom means you are unobstructed in living your life as you choose. Anything less is a form of slavery." – Wayne Dyer

"Don't trade in your authenticity for approval." – Purehappylife.com

"Authenticity is the daily practice of letting go of who we think we're supposed to be and embracing who we are." – Brene Brown

"Authenticity is a collection of choices that we have to make every day. It's about the choice to show up and be real. The choice to be honest. The choice to let our true selves be seen". – Brene Brown, Make the choice today to be YOU. [Is this a separate quote or your own thought?]

"Shine with all you have, when someone tries to blow you out, just take their oxygen and burn brighter." – Katelyn Irons

"Authenticity is the most attractive garment you could ever wear." – Unknown

"By choosing to be our most authentic and loving self, we leave a trail of magic everywhere we go." – Quotead[d?]icts.com

"Authenticity is knowing who you are and being brave enough to live it."
– Pinterest.com

"To be yourself in a world that is constantly trying to make you something else is the greatest accomplishment." – Ralph Waldo Emerson

## Chapter Five

# Think like A Victor

### *Stop Complaining*

*"Summing it all up, friends, I'd say you'll do best by filling your minds and meditating on things true, noble, reputable, authentic, compelling, gracious – the best, not the worst; the beautiful, not the ugly; things to praise, not things to curse. Put into practice what you learned from me, what you heard and saw and realized. Do that, and God, who makes everything work together, will work you into his most excellent                                                        harmonies."*
— *Philippians 4:8-9 the Message (MSG)*

As I began to write this chapter, I experienced writer's block and I couldn't convey what I wanted to say, so, for about a week and a half, I didn't write. I listened to different audios on the mind. I remembered that I had purchased this book two weeks prior entitled "The Power of Now" by Eckart Tolle.

As I begin to listen to the audio on this book, my thoughts started to become clear and I was ready to write. So many great subjects to talk about, where do I begin?

Growing up I had never heard of "the victor" - "victim", maybe, but definitely not anything close to victorious. I was victorious in my mind, but with depressing things: I had won a gold medal for being first place as a negative thinker. That was my prize, and I wore it very well.

I wasn't cultured on how to think like a victor. I assumed my way through life as a follower of the noise in my mind and it led me to a place of confinement - a prisoner of my own ability to mimic what I saw and heard. Having the desire to break free from all the mental torment, but having no clue how to begin to clean out the rooms of my mind, I had created many compartments. Each compartment was filled with just enough to keep me a prisoner. I met people along the way that helped me remain in that state of mind *the toxic friends, the unfaithful boyfriends, the liars, the cheaters, and the gossipers*. They all played a strategic part in my life and helped me to get where I am today: free from everybody's opinion of whom and what I should have been.

It wasn't easy breaking free from this mental hold I placed on myself. Observing people whose opinions I deemed more important than mine *instead of treasuring myself*, it was easy for me to accept what they thought, since I had been living my life according to their beliefs and judgments; so continuing on this downward spiral felt right.

Because of how I was raised, I nurtured this fragile shell from childhood into a tough "I don't need anybody" attitude. I approached everything and everybody with this unidentified pride. Whatever I needed to be at that moment, I could easily play the role. After all, I had been auditioning for it all my life; I was just being my normal self; others would view it as…well, you fill in the blank.

I was a lot of things back then, and being a victor wasn't one of them. Well, at least that's not how I looked at it. I had a lot of strengths but I used them selfishly to manipulate for my own gain in getting whatever I wanted. Now I know that may sound arrogant, but I was trying to survive the only way I knew how. I adopted this attitude for a tough and vocal person who displayed no discretion with her tongue. It was sharp and could pierce through your feelings without a second thought. Hurt people hurt people. It took me a long time to realize that I didn't have to be that person who was self-possessed by her own untrained mind.

I knew I needed help. I began to detox my mind, which was life-changing. I started eliminating all negatives - thoughts, words, and people -from my life. I ate a full meal each day of positivity and inspiring affirmations. I started walking, and I used that time to commune with the only one who made an escape for me. Some days I laughed, and other days I thanked Him for growth; sometimes I cried because I could see the change in my life, and I felt so alive. I was so glad I had made a decision to clean up my mind; I started speaking life into myself by renewing my mind. This was by far one of the best decisions I had ever made: becoming a "new me". No more road rage, no anger, no loud talking. I had a calmness that was unexplainable - I knew I was changing from the Inside. And to me, for the first time, I was acting like a victor and not a victim.

What is a victor? A person who defeats? A winner? Champion? A conqueror? That's who *you* are, regardless of all the noise in your mind. You are not your mind and you are not your thoughts. You are a creator: anything you want, you have the power to manifest it.

Tolle's book "The Power of Now" has given a new meaning on how I should think, and that I am totally in control of my thoughts. I want to expound on this book and how I understood it, and how I used it to help me think like a victor. This is my understanding of the book and my judgments.

For many years, my thoughts had influenced every area of my life: either by living in the past or expanding too far into the future, I was not quite in the present. For most Americans, that's where we reside in our thoughts. There is this imbalance that causes us to live outside of our natural self, which causes us to be unhappy, depressed, with low self-esteem, feeling unworthy, and many other negative emotions on a daily basis.

When I moved to High Point, North Carolina in March of 1997, I started attending this church where I had given my life to the Lord. I was faithful, and so eager to learn about God! I was excited and of course, *still longing for love and affection and clinging to anybody who showed interest.* I started communicating with an older man in the church. Being young and naive, *I was 27* at the time, but age is only a number right? During one of our conversations I accepted an invitation to his house. There, once again, I was taken advantage of. He denied it, and I blamed myself for going to his home and allowing it to happen. I still replay those events in my head over and over, continually telling myself *"it's your fault, you should have never gone over there."* I sometimes wonder if I will ever get over those devastating events. Why do I keep blaming myself for other people's behavior?

Over the years, I have done some embarrassing things I'm ashamed of, and the guilt has kept me a prisoner in my mind. I have slept with men I knew weren't right for me. I have been with other people's husbands and boyfriends. I made excuses why I did it - the noise in my mind confirmed it was ok. I didn't't have any self-respect for myself, so why would I respect other people's relationships? I was still searching for love everywhere. I contemplated whether or not I should add this in my book - I was afraid of exposing some of the darkest places of my life and the shame and guilt I was feeling on the inside. I was ready to be set free of the very thing that was holding me captive.

No matter how hard I tried not to act in that manner, the more I did. Not knowing how to respect myself, I placed my worth in a man's hand. I allowed them to treat me like trash and talk to me like I was nothing. The noise in my head told me I deserved to be treated like that so why are you complaining. I have engaged in promiscuous sexual intercourse with men I barely knew; searching for love. I didn't know how to respect myself. If they liked me I was down for it most of the time.

My behavior was getting the best of me and inwardly, I felt cheap and trashy. Now; *let me clear something up.* Although that was my behavior, I never had a one night stand, never slept with anybody off the street, or sold my body (*not by the world's standards anyway*). Everybody has their own beliefs about who they are, but in my mind, I was a bad girl who had done bad things. The noise in my mind was so loud it caused me to think I had done the unthinkable; when I was only responding to the cards I had been dealt.

One day I had to grow up. I'm a mother now, and that type of behavior isn't tolerated when raising a daughter. Even after having my daughter, I struggled with men and giving them my most precious gift: my body. I still wanted so badly to be loved. I tried so hard to do things right by God's standards, but somehow I couldn't't do it. The harder I tried, the more I messed up, and the sexual relationships with men increased.

I'm not that person anymore: the thoughts still come, but I'm a lot stronger now and I no longer listen to them.

I've experienced too many times where my mind would take me so far in the future that I would get upset about something that hadn't even happened yet. *Ever felt that way especially when it comes to*: relationships, finances or bills?

Just recently, I opened a bill that was due 3 months in advance and I got upset because the amount of the bill had increased, and at that moment I didn't have the money in my account, but then I immediately reminded myself to stay in the moment, that it's three months away and that I will have the money when I need it. This is what we often do - expand mentally so far into the future; it steals our peace and makes us depressed or stressed about something you have no control over. Stay in the moment.

When I wasn't thinking in the future, I was living in the past. Why was I still responding to all of those outdated stories? It's because the mind deliberately concentrates on negativity. We wake up to negative thoughts, we have negative thoughts during the day and we go to bed with negative thoughts, to do it all over again the next morning. It's a never ending cycle.

I was reminded of this scripture that helped me stay focused:

*"Give your entire attention to what God is doing right now, and don't get worked up about what may or may*

*not happen tomorrow. God will help you deal with whatever hard things come up when the time comes. "*
— Matthew 6:34 "The Message" (MSG), King James Bible

Here is another way to put it:

*Take therefore no thought for the morrow: for the morrow shall take thought for the things of itself*

it helps me stay in the now and keeps my mind from wandering all over the place. A wandering mind keeps you unhappy and stressed out. It's not what you go through that makes you unhappy - it's the *thoughts* of what you're going through that makes you unhappy. Yesterday has been redeemed, you can't get it back. Today is non-returnable; you're in it. You can't forfeit it now, and tomorrow isn't guaranteed, so live in today, the present, and be happy. We're not what we think about all day - we are only defeated if we think we are - and the only limitations we have is OURSELVES. Think like an overcomer, act like an overcomer, be an overcomer.

When you start to take on this victor image, some will think you're being anti-social; it's not that at all. Some will be offended by your new positive outlook on life. Don't worry, be happy. The funny thing is, when you no longer hiss, rattle, and slither in the grass of gossip and hearsay as the old you, your listeners won't understand the sudden change and they will try and engage you in the gossip again. This time around, your eyes will be opened to a whole new way of living; separation is necessary so you can complete the process. I know you probably read that above statement and thought, "wow, she acted like a snake metaphorically", well, don't be too alarmed, you did too. You had your hissing and slithering moments too: you covered it well under all the makeup, the lashes, the press-on nails and the hair extensions, or the six pack abs, the big biceps and triceps and that unforgettable smile.

When we over-indulge in one area we unknowingly cover up weaknesses, frustrations, desires, or feelings of inadequacy or incompetence through self-gratification or immeasurable excellence in another area.

Overcompensation is something I did, covering up deficiencies and limitations. I had so many, I just acted accordingly. My limitations were me; I staged my own dreams and happiness by chasing something I would have never caught. I existed fully in self-blame and self-criticism far too long. I had every excuse to be pessimistic and feel as though the world owed me something. Although I am a Christian, I had a victim mentality and rarely wanted to take responsibility for where I was in life. It was easier to play the "blame game", so I did, for many years.

Now that I'm beginning to think like a victor, my appearance has changed. I no longer care what anyone thinks about what I wear, and the tight fitting clothing I would have never worn, I wear gracefully. I style my hair any way I like now; you may see it long, short, curly, or straight. It's my choice, and I feel good about my positive change. My confidence is contagious and it affects the people around me. Most people noticed the positive change and some said, *"you seem happier, more at ease, like you're more relaxed, and less in control."* I had to learn how to relax and not be so serious, give up the macho attitude and allow people room to make errors before I had written them off. There was no room for second chances *although I needed them the most.* I shifted my attention and energy to being positive and looking for the best in all people. I love thinking like a victor because it feels good. I can smile now without having a reason; I can hear something negative or something I disagree with, and my response is uplifting to allow more chances to do it again. I calmly respond to negativity now, turning it into an opportunity.

Most days I feel like I have "Superwoman" written on my chest and that I can conquer the world. And today, I can. I'm more than a conqueror, and all things are working together for my good. See you in the next chapter.

## Just a few quotes to ponder:

"Go for it now, the future is promised to no one." — Wayne Dyer

"Never underestimate your power to change yourself; never overestimate your power to change others." — Wayne Dyer

"The only limits you have are the limits you believe." —Wayne Dyer

"My circumstances do not make me what I am, they reveal who I have chosen to be." —Wayne Dyer

"All blame is a waste of time, no matter how much fault you find with another, it will not change you." — Wayne Dyer

"Simply be the qualities you seek in others." — Wayne Dyer

Chapter Six

# I Found Freedom in the Noise

*I Am Freedom*

*"We are destroying sophisticated arguments and every exalted and proud thing that sets itself up against the [true] knowledge of God, and we are taking every thought and purpose captive to the obedience of Christ" — 2 Corinthians 10:5 Amplified Bible (AMP)*

I remember researching online, looking for something about morals and how to change. Boy, did I find what I was looking for! My life changed in a matter of a few months. I went from "stinking thinking" to "victorious thinking". I had found confidence that literally turned my whole life around. I began to adjust how I was thinking. I was so enthusiastic for change; I would have done anything constructive to get to that place. Now, this didn't happen overnight, but I was so ready for something different that I spent at least half a day, every day, on making the necessary adjustments on changing the way I was thinking.

I remember being on You-tube, trying to find a way to increase my credit score, and I clicked on a link that forever changed my life. I began to start watching a man named Wayne Dyer. Who would have ever thought that listening to all the wisdom he had would lead me to not only changing my thought process but also allow me to learn how to create anything I desired out of a place of my higher self? And in that place, I was reminded after all these years that, "I'm a spiritual being having a human experience". As I begin to tell my story of how I found freedom in the noise, I learned it from listening to Wayne Dyer and some other great people. I will list different quotes and statements that have transformed my life within this chapter.

One of the first things I learned was that I was in control of my thoughts, and that I had the power to change them. That was the million dollar concept for me and it transformed my life - it was worth more than anything I had ever known at that moment. I had such a hunger for change I started eating everything Dyer was saying and started applying it to my life. "The beginning of wisdom is this: Get wisdom and whatever you get, get insight" *Proverbs 4:7, New International Version.*

I started reprogramming my mind with affirmations.

Affirmations are, in short, an effective way to plant positive messages into your subconscious. I realized that I had already started doing those years prior, but I didn't know there was a name for it. Throughout my house I have affirmations on my mirrors and doors. God *always* has a plan, even when we don't recognize it!

I heard Wayne Dyer use these three words and how we should use them in our lives to make the necessary changes: negativity, judgment, and imbalance. I applied his concepts, and the results were phenomenal. I want to share with you how I use them as a guide to change; these are my words and thoughts.

The first is *negativity*. It is defined as the expression of criticism of or pessimism about something or someone, lacking positive or affirmative qualities, (such as enthusiasm, interest, or optimism). This was a big one for me because when I started this life changing journey I had never realized how negative my thoughts were until I began to replace them with the opposite. Not only were my thoughts negative, my actions were as well. It was really easy to engage in a gossiping conversation without thought. What was implanted inside of me was coming out of me. You can't get something from someone if they don't have it to give; gossiping, backbiting, lying, cheating, stealing etc., all of that was subconsciously rooted in me, and when that energy showed up, we connected quickly.

Have you ever wondered why you attract the people you do? I was curious too, being single and unconsciously attracting men who were unavailable, angry, unstable, liars, and already in relationships. Looking externally, I couldn't comprehend why this kept happening until I educated myself on the mind. When I understood it, I was able to apply the teachings I had learned. We should always try and see the best in everyone even if they don't see it in you.

Here are some quotes that stuck with me:
"How people treat you is their karma, how you react is yours."
"See the light in others, and treat them as if that is all you

see." "Change the way you see things and the things you see will change."

"Loving people live in a loving world, hostile people live in a hostile world. Same world".

Simply be the qualities you seek in others.

Next is *judgment*. It is an opinion or decision that is based on careful thought. The ability to judge, make a decision, or form an opinion objectively, authoritatively, and wisely, especially in matters affecting action. This seems to be dominant in all of our lives: we live every day with some type of judgment toward someone, and it's mostly negative judgment. We can't help it, it's not our fault; we were raised in an environment that judged everything. This is one reason why we conflict with the noise on the inside. Social media, television and the communities around us taught us well. But that can change, and it starts with a decision to change how you see others. "When you judge another, you do not define them, you define yourself". We have to limit the chatter. Judgment comes from within. About this, Dyer goes further, stating:

"Don't believe everything you think."
"Conflict or judgment cannot survive without your participation."
"To sit in judgment of those things which you perceive to be wrong or imperfect is to be one more person who is part of judgment, evil, or imperfection."
If it isn't edifying, don't share your input.

Lastly is *imbalance*. It's a state or condition in which different things do not occur in equal or proper amounts, or lack of proportion or relation between corresponding things. Here is a good example between your true nature and the flesh; the flesh lusts against the Spirit and the Spirit against the flesh, and these are contrary to one another, so that you do not do the things that you wish, and depending on how much time you spend with each of them, one is coming out on top. When you get to that place and you're dissatisfied with all the noise that is still controlling everything that you do, you better act like you're running a sprint, running to get there in the least amount of time. This is a good place to take the short distance, typically as a way of quickly reaching a target or goal. The faster the better - we have no more time to waste. Too many years have been stolen from you already.

Transforming your mind brings balance to your life: not all the material things you possess, but truly understanding who you are as a person. Everything God is, you're an exact copy of. "We are not human beings in search of a spiritual experience, we are spiritual beings immersed in a human experience", Dyer states. He goes on: "You are always a valuable, worthwhile human being – not because anybody says so, not because you're successful, not because you make a lot of money, but because you decided to believe it and not for any other reason." "We are not our bodies, our possessions, or our careers. Who we are is Divine Love and that is infinite." "Raise yourself to the level of energy where you are the light you seek, where you are the happiness you desire, where you are the love you feel is missing, where you are the unlimited abundance you crave."

I used these quotes daily to help transform my life and it has made me a far better mother, woman, entrepreneur, author, coach, and teacher. Besides, reading all of these wonderful quotes and affirmations, I cannot forget to add the most important piece to the puzzle: that is, the Creator of all things, He is the source of all my supply, He is unquestionably and positively the beginning and MY end. Everything starts with Him. He is known as God of the entire universe.

I remember reading this in the book of Genesis: that I was created in His image and likeness, which makes me capable of becoming anything I wanted to be. An image (*in this context*) is an exact replica of something; when I read that it inspired me to go a little deeper and wanted to learn more about who I was. An exact replica that's powerful and that's who we are. I'm not my body, I'm not who people call me, I'm not what they said I was going to be, I'm not a failure, I'm not a screw-up, I'm not someone's problem, but *"I am all that I am"*. And that's everything good, everything that was/is good, God did it. We are the most powerful creatures on earth, we were put together so delicately (our Spirit). Surely He wouldn't just place it in anything that has no value. When He created this outer shell we call our bodies, he made it fearfully and wonderfully. God is so amazing that He can just take two simple words which have such a powerful meaning. Unlike us, we don't always grasp the meaning of something unless it's spelled out in great detail, like *fearfully and wonderfully*. I wonder what God was really saying, "look at it like this. I want you to take a moment and show in great detail about something you love; for me let me customize the car of my dreams, build it from start to finish, just like you want it, imagine this, something that makes you go into deep thought puts a smile on your face or leaves you with a 'WOW' I love this car...

*2016 Lexus IS 250*
*The first-ever IS Turbo features an exhilarating 241-horsepower\**
*turbocharged engine, a highly rigid chassis with track-tuned*
*suspension and an 8-speed Sport Direct-Shift transmission. 18-*
*inch mesh alloy wheels with 225/40R18 (front), 255/35R18 (rear)*
*Black Exterior, with red and black Interior seats, Keyless Entry &*
*Start, Power Front Seats, Dual Zone Climate Control, a Power*
*Sunroof, a Back Up Camera, Cruise Control, Bluetooth, Voice*
*Control, an Auto-Dimming Rear View Mirror, and Home Link."*

See the difference that just gave me life? When you can feel or resonate with something, it becomes real to you. That's how your body was constructed: created top of the line, every detail of this outer shell made perfectly. No imperfections, but fearfully, wonderfully made, so it is very important that you take care of it. For instance, sometimes we let other people drive our most valued possession (you know that custom-made brand new car, and how they didn't take care of it, or we didn't take care of it because we didn't know the value of it? Sometimes that's because our mind doesn't recognize valuable good. Until we are reprogrammed to think positively and know that you are not just a body but a spiritual being, it is only then that your entire life will change.

As you begin to go through this metamorphosis (*from caterpillar to butterfly*) there will be some resistance from your old self and from people closest to you. That's okay; keep moving forward. All of this is designed to happen; it keeps you focused on what's in

THE POWER OF A SILENT THOUGHT

front of you. As I began my journey from caterpillar to butterfly, I encountered some resistance from people I would have never thought would change and I was okay with that, because I was determined this time not to go back. They could no longer pull my string in their direction.  After weeks of being reprogrammed, I immediately saw the increase in my energy level, and, not long after that, I had confidence that was out of this world, and it felt great. I was finally moving into my natural self and, for some reason, that irritated some people, and I didn't care. One of my friends said this to me during this time.

"People receive "change" as arrogance, selfishness, and being anti-social sometimes. But the moment you begin to love yourself and get reacquainted with who you really are, that you never knew, your world will explode with greatness, only people who are ignorant of God's great change in you, will not receive it! Keep exposing yourself to new people, places, and things. OUT with the old, IN with the new! Congrats to your new happy place." – Janella Purvis

Don't get discouraged and crawl back in your shell when people don't embrace the new you. You are the most important person in your life. If you control your thought, you will control how you feel.

As I'm writing this last chapter, there is still a lot of noise going on in my mind about "why this" and "why that". One thing for sure - you cannot control what people do. Although it's still a lot of rumbling and echoing, I made a conscious decision to take control of my thoughts and I refuse to let them have dominion over me. I'm the co-creator over this house, and I choose to be HAPPY! I finally fell in love with *me*. I love the new me and it shows up everywhere I go. Take a moment and make a decision today to change your life. All that is required is a decision.

Remember this: "Yesterday has been redeemed, Today is non-returnable, Tomorrow isn't guaranteed" – *unknown*

Start today…Changing your mind is a journey of a lifetime!

**She is the reason!!**

# About the Author

Kristen Pittman is a Dillon, South Carolina native currently living and working in Greensboro, North Carolina. She is currently working as a Billing Healthcare Professional, and although she loves the interaction with her patients, she has always had a heart for empowering and inspiring people to become their absolute best. Even as a young child, she had a passion for helping people to become conscious of their unlimited potential and their unseen possibilities.

Kristen is the mother of one daughter, Krishada (Kay) who is a high school senior and will be going to NCCU in the fall of 2017. She enjoys cooking and traveling. Her faith in God is strong, and she contributes that to her willingness to encourage the people she encounters to be aware of their thoughts. She loves the challenge of assisting them in rewiring the mind.

Kristen's strong desire for mental development and her aspiration for understanding the way the mind works lead her to learn the fundamentals of the conscious and subconscious mind. She learned the principles of life coaching with a concentration in personal development and spirituality. Life coaching helps you reach a goal or make profound changes in your life. Kristen's main goal is to transform your life, help you download the necessary information to make a lasting change; she not only wants to motivate, educate, and inspire you, but stimulates you to live a successful life. Transformational coaching is essential to a well-balanced life.

Kristen attained three certificates: Public Speaking, Life Coaching, and Motivational Speaking. She also holds several Associate Degrees: Radiography from Forsyth Technical Community College; Microcomputer Information Science from Commonwealth College; and Business Administration from Guilford Technical Community College. Kristen is additionally certified in Phlebotomy from Guilford Technical Community College and is American Registry of Radiologic Technologists (ARRT) certified in North Carolina.

**Kristen's Contact Information**
Pittman8170@gmail.com
positiveselftalkforum@gmail.com
www.mindsetdevelopment.net
(336)-410-3145

* Author, Spiritual Coach and Personal Development Coach * Motivational Speaker and Entrepreneur *

www.ingramcontent.com/pod-product-compliance
Lightning Source LLC
Chambersburg PA
CBHW060204290526
45789CB00003B/1159